Seeing Through Internet Hoaxes

Fiona Young-Brown

Cavendish Square

New York

Published in 2019 by Cavendish Square Publishing, LLC
243 5th Avenue, Suite 136, New York, NY 10016

Website: cavendishsq.com

This publication represents the opinions and views of the author based on his or her
personal experience, knowledge, and research. The information in this book serves
as a general guide only. The author and publisher have used their best efforts in
preparing this book and disclaim liability rising directly or indirectly from the use
and application of this book.

All websites were available and accurate when this book was sent to press.

Cataloging-in-Publication Data

Names: Young-Brown, Fiona.
Title: Seeing through internet hoaxes / Fiona Young-Brown.
Description: New York : Cavendish Square, 2019. | Series: News literacy |
Includes glossary and index.
Identifiers: ISBN 9781502641496 (pbk.) | ISBN 9781502641502 (library bound) |
ISBN 9781502641519 (ebook)
Subjects: LCSH: Computer fraud--Juvenile literature. |
Computer crimes--Juvenile literature.
Classification: LCC HV6773.15.C56 Y68 2019 | DDC 613.6--dc23

Editorial Director: David McNamara
Editor: Caitlyn Miller
Copy Editor: Lisa Goldstein
Associate Art Director: Alan Sliwinski
Designer: Amy Greenan
Production Coordinator: Karol Szymczuk
Photo Research: J8 Media

Printed in the United States of America

CONTENTS

English school children reenact the famous spaghetti tree hoax that aired on British television in the 1950s.

What Is an Internet Hoax?

I n 1957, a British television program showed a video of people gathering the spaghetti harvest in Switzerland. The farming family walked from tree to tree, filling baskets with the long strands of pasta that were apparently growing there. The date that the program aired might be the first clue to whether or not it was true: April 1. The spaghetti tree hoax was an elaborate and now-famous April Fool's Day prank. One of the reasons it was so successful was that so few people in the United Kingdom knew where pasta came from. So when they saw people picking it from trees, why shouldn't they believe it?

The overwhelming popularity of the internet means such a story would probably not be believed were it to air

The internet is an essential resource, but hoaxes spread quickly online.

today. It is much easier to check how truthful something is, and of course, we are now much more familiar with international foods and cultures. Nevertheless, the internet has become a fertile garden for hoaxes and fake news.

A hoax is any sort of deception. It can be either malicious or humorous in its intent. Looking back, the example of the spaghetti tree is quite funny. Nobody would be hurt by the joke. But other hoaxes, as we shall read, can be more dangerous. Some, such as the spaghetti tree, are created by the media. Others are not created by the media, but newspapers report the story as truth, thereby spreading the falsehood. Journalists, too, are victims of the hoax.

As internet usage has grown in popularity in the past few decades, we have entered a new information age. Younger generations have grown up in a world where they feel perfectly comfortable using technology. Meanwhile, older generations have learned how to integrate it into everyday life. We have access to a wide variety of news programming whenever we want it. However, the internet has also changed the face of news in more ways than accessibility. Anyone can put information online. This has given rise to the concept of citizen journalism. Whereas we used to rely on trained newspaper reporters to provide us with updates of local and global events, now anyone can report or create news.

We can create photos, videos, and stories as they happen. We can then share them via blogs and social media. Those stories can take on a life of their own as they spread. In some cases, such citizen journalism can spread awareness of an issue and can work collaboratively with mainstream news media. In December 2010, a series of protests began in Tunisia. The demonstrations eventually caused the president to resign and the country to hold

Thousands of people, like those pictured here in Egypt, protested against their governments in 2010 and 2011, in what came to be known as the Arab Spring.

The skull of Piltdown Man was "found" in Sussex in 1912.
In the 1950s, it was proven to be an elaborate hoax.

THE PILTDOWN MAN

Hoax news stories existed long before the internet. In fact, one of the most famous and most successful took place in 1912. It wasn't revealed as a fake until more than forty years later.

An amateur archaeologist claimed to have found some early skeletal remains near the village of Piltdown in southern England. This Piltdown Man, as the remains became known, was an estimated five hundred thousand years old, making him the missing link between apes and humans. Scientists viewed the discovery as a huge step forward in their understanding of evolution. The skull and those who found it became known around the world.

But it was all a fake. By the 1950s, new technology allowed scientists to date remains more accurately. Tests showed that the bone fragments were only about fifty thousand years old. What's more, the bones were not from the same creature. Someone had combined human and ape bones to create an elaborate forgery. They had even carefully filed down the teeth so that they looked less like those of an animal.

Even today, researchers are still trying to decide who was behind the trickery. Most think it was the amateur archaeologist, working alone, who managed to fool so many experts. His Piltdown Man remains one of the twentieth century's greatest hoaxes.

democratic elections. The success of the protesters led to similar protests in neighboring countries in 2011. This series of uprisings became known as the Arab Spring. The Arab Spring protests gained a global audience thanks to locals sharing events as they happened.

On the other hand, there can be a downside to anyone being able to spread information. As we shall read, it has made the spreading of hoaxes much easier.

New Technology, New Hoaxes

As internet technology has advanced, so have other forms of digital technologies. We can now shoot photos or videos on our cell phones. Not so long ago, manipulating an image or video would have required a lot of sophisticated equipment. Now, editing programs such as Photoshop make it much cheaper and easier to change what we see. Demands for photographic proof of a story can now be answered with digital manipulation. These fake photos can then make spreading a story even easier.

In addition to technological advances, there are other factors related to the widespread use of the internet that contribute to the spreading of false information. People from around the world can now come together, united by common interests. In some instances, this is a good thing. People with specific illnesses or those who live in remote areas can find friends like them. At the same time, it has allowed fringe groups, hate groups, terrorists, and so on to create networks. They can spread hoaxes, and in doing so, help to reinforce their beliefs. The validation of

IN THE WORDS OF AN EXPERT

According to Jack Speer, a newscaster with National Public Radio:

> Fake news is to me something that is patently untrue. It is spread more now via the Internet than in the past ... You want to look at the source—where are you getting your news from? Are you getting your news from a credible media outlet? As a consumer, you have to be somewhat skeptical about why this is out there.

Speer is saying that fake news is spreading rapidly, thanks to the internet. It is up to readers to make sure that our news is coming from a credible, or trusted, organization. Though not all fake news involves hoaxes, all hoaxes are fake news. Some fake news is a misrepresentation of the facts to suit a particular bias rather than an outright lie. For example, a news source might take a quote out of context or might partially report an issue to suit an argument. Savvy readers use the same critical thinking skills to spot fake news and hoaxes.

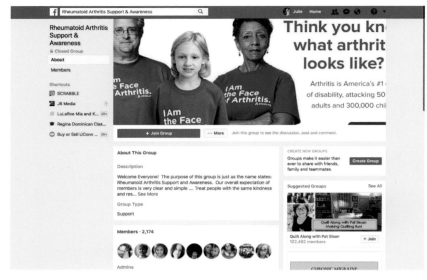

This online group for arthritis sufferers is an example of the internet being used to do good.

knowing there are others who think the same way they do gives these groups a sense of increased power.

Why Hoaxes Matter

Hoaxes and fake news can seem harmless, but that's not always the case. Some hoaxes can lead to very real emergency situations. For example, when false information has been spread about a medical issue, that can cause major health problems. Vaccinations have become a controversial issue, with thousands of people continuing to share claims that certain vaccinations can kill or cause autism. Both claims have been repeatedly debunked by medical professionals, scientific researchers, and fact-checkers. Still, they persist. Vaccinations prevent deadly diseases such as cervical cancer and measles.

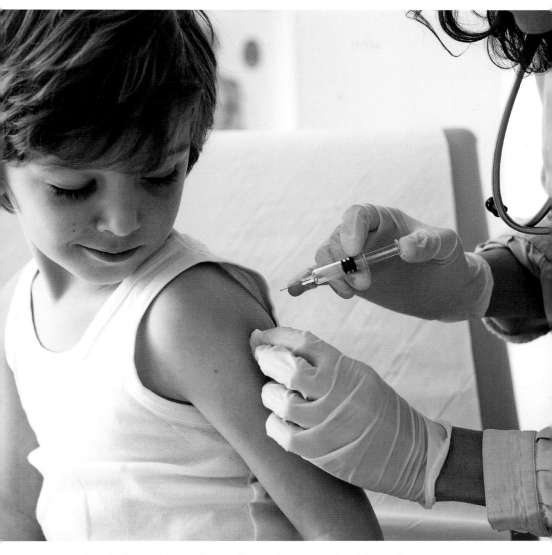

Misinformation about "unsafe" vaccinations has spread over the internet, putting kids at risk of illness.

A vital part of news literacy is learning which online information is true and which is not.

How many people could potentially die of these diseases because of dangerous and false information online?

A recent study by researchers at Stanford University looked at students in middle and high school to see how well they could interpret what they encounter on the internet. The results were quite shocking. The researchers found that most students are poorly equipped in media literacy. Very few know how to evaluate an online source for accuracy. While many would deny the oft-repeated phrase, "If it's on the internet, it must be true," many were easily misled. As long as a website looked professional, the students generally accepted the information on the site without question. If students did look at the "About Us" page to verify the organization, they were all too willing to accept what they saw at face value.

Rarely do students check an organization's background or the sources quoted in an article. At the same time, young people will share photos and videos without considering that they might have been altered. One example widely given is a photo of misshapen flowers with the claim that they are growing in Fukushima, Japan—the area affected by a nuclear power leak in 2011. The claim implies that radiation from the nuclear accident is causing mutations in the wildlife. Yet there is nothing accompanying the image other than an unsubstantiated claim.

Researchers also found that students did not understand how bias might affect what they were reading. For example, is the article really sponsored content being presented as news? Is the publication presenting the story heavily biased politically, and if so, how might that affect their reporting of an issue? This lack of media literacy is not just limited to school-age students. College students who participated in the study were also unable to tell the difference between an accepted mainstream organization and a fringe source.

Inaccurately analyzing a piece of information or accepting it at face value increases the risk of spreading inaccurate and possibly dangerous information. Maureen Paschal is a librarian who teaches students how to recognize fake news and hoaxes on the internet. She says, "The only reliable way to protect citizens from fake news, alternate facts, or hate groups is for all of us to learn how to navigate digital information with discernment and skepticism."

Pictures of a strange daisy were spread online as "proof" of the damage being done by nuclear radiation in Fukushima, Japan. Yet there was never any evidence that radiation was to blame.

Characteristics of an Internet Hoax

I n order to better understand and avoid internet
hoaxes, it is important to learn more about them.
Librarian Paul Piper is a professor who specializes
in internet media literacy. Piper says, "Misinformation
on the Internet is, and will always be, a problem. One
of the attributes of the Internet—the fact that nearly
anyone can publish on it—creates an environment of
freedom and simultaneously an environment that lacks
quality control." He says that it is the responsibility
of internet users to check the facts about online
content and evaluate if that content is real. It is, of
course, important to be able to do this with any type

of information. That could be an email, a story in a print newspaper or magazine, or TV news. Media literacy is a form of problem solving, just like in math or science class.

Sharing a story from a print magazine takes time. Yet social media makes it all too easy to click and share with little more information than the headline. But when people click "share" without thinking, they could be spreading a piece of fake news. That's why it is so important to take the time to do a little research and spot the signs of a hoax. There are many different types of hoaxes online. Some of these are detailed below.

Spoofs and Satirical Sites

Some websites are set up to be parodies or spoofs of a particular site or topic. The content is often humorous and so absurd that it could not possibly be real. For example, there are several spoof tourist sites about Mankato in Minnesota. One talks about how underground steam pits mean that the temperature never drops below 70 degrees Fahrenheit (21 degrees Celsius). You can even visit the original Castle Dracula! It sounds wonderful ... except for the fact that we know winters in Minnesota are cold and snowy. Furthermore, Dracula's castle is thousands of miles away in Romania. While fun to read, the site is obviously intended as a joke.

Satirical websites are another type of site where the humor is usually more subtle. Probably the best known of these is the *Onion*, which pokes fun at society through local, national, and international stories. Although the site's tagline is "America's Finest News Source," one glance at the site and it is fairly clear that this is not real. Stories range from the obviously absurd ("Zombie Nutritionist Recommends All-Brain Diet") to satirical commentary on current affairs ("Resigned Climate Scientists Say to Just Enjoy Next 20 Years As Much As You Can"). Readers familiar with the *Onion* will know that the articles are not to be regarded as truthful. However, individual stories can look quite realistic. An unsuspecting web surfer might come across one through a Google search and mistakenly think it is real.

Spoof news stories, such as this one, are funny but are clearly not true.

Some sites are completely fictional, based upon information from a popular book or video game. For example, geography students might know that there is no such Eastern European country as Ruritania. But the website, based upon the made-up nation named in a nineteenth-century novel, looks quite realistic and could be mistaken for genuine. Some book characters even have their own blogs, set up either by fans or by the author as a marketing tool. These are designed to entertain the reader.

Malicious Sites

In contrast to humorous hoaxes, there are the malicious types of hoax websites. Many of these present themselves as genuine. A closer look reveals that they are anything but. The intent behind many such sites is to deliberately spread false information. Librarian Paul Piper gives the example of a site claiming to be about Martin Luther King Jr. It is actually operated by a white-supremacist

It can be difficult to separate fake news from the truth. The first step is thinking critically about what you read.

group that wants to spread unfair lies about the man. There are also a number of false Native American sites that instead attack traditional Native American culture. Others might present themselves as very academic sites, with many links and reports. They may even have an important-sounding title. However, the information they provide contains many false facts to support their own harmful claims. Commonly found examples of topics covered by such sites are Holocaust denial or the claim that AIDS does not really exist.

The road to a federal infrastructure package begins with a Highway Trust Fund fix

Sponsored content, like this story, can be biased and misleading.

Biased Sites and Sponsored Content

Some news sites are heavily biased toward one political leaning or another. They are not always malicious in their intent (although some most definitely are). Nevertheless, they can still be very misleading. Supporters of the same political side might argue that such sites are simply presenting "the facts." Opponents will argue the opposite—that they are distorting the "real" truth.

Both sides are allowing their own bias to influence the way they report a story and may be distorting some facts or taking quotes out of context. This is why it is particularly important to know who is behind a site. It is also a good idea to read several different outlets' versions of an incident to see which common threads link them all.

Another type of article to notice is not a true hoax. It can be misleading, though, and so it is good to recognize it. It is called sponsored content and is becoming more and more common. A company will pay for an article. Usually, the phrase "sponsored content" can be found somewhere at the top of the page, but it may be in very small letters. The article itself will look just like a normal news article. The difference is that it is designed to advertise a particular product. For example, it might be a report that claims one skin cream is better than all the others. The goal of the article is to encourage more people to buy that product. While this in itself is not always a hoax or fake news, recognizing biased content is part of developing the skill set to recognize hoaxes.

Social Media Hoaxes

Hoaxes are not just limited to websites. While some are spread via social media, others may be created on social media. One person might write a Tweet or a Facebook post expressing an opinion or suggesting a personal theory regarding an event. People share the post until it goes viral, taking on a life of its own, and changing slightly with each share. Soon it is no longer one person's belief but

WHY DO PEOPLE FALL FOR HOAXES?

It is likely that everyone has at least once believed a story later proven to be a fake. Even after a story is shown to be false, many people still believe parts of it to be true. It has planted a seed of doubt in our minds that persists.

Scientists at Ghent University in Belgium believe that our cognitive ability influences how we react to hoaxes and fake news, much more so than our political beliefs or open-mindedness. Cognitive ability is a person's ability to process information and solve problems. It can be strengthened or weakened by a number of factors, including age and education.

Meanwhile, researchers at the University of Toronto have found that the more often something is repeated, the more people will believe it. Our brains can mistake frequency of hearing something for truth. What's more, if something is repeated enough, even after being told that it is incorrect, we still tend to believe it.

Some say that people believe fake news because they want to. But it is much more complicated. Repeated exposure and our own problem-solving abilities can trick our brains into believing anything.

something accepted as fact. For example, a man in Texas saw a large number of buses in town one day and thought it was odd. Later, he read that the president was giving a speech in town, and so the man thought that the buses must be full of protesters. He posted pictures on Twitter. Within a day it had been shared more than 350,000 times on Facebook and more than 16,000 times on Twitter. In reality, the buses were bringing people to a conference. The rumor of protests had already spread far and wide. The man later said that he was too busy to fact-check before posting.

This photo from a 2014 story about Robert Mugabe was actually taken in 2009.

Altered Images

Other internet hoaxes are little more than a picture, either taken out of context or digitally altered. Modern technology makes it very easy to alter an image, whether for humorous results or for more questionable motives. In 2014, there were rumors about the health of Zimbabwean president Robert Mugabe, so readers were no doubt relieved to see a picture of him, looking healthy and smiling, when he stepped from a plane after a meeting in Singapore. It was soon revealed, however, that the pictures used were actually several years old and related to a completely different meeting in Ethiopia. As soon as the origin of the photo was revealed, it fueled more rumors about his health. Why not use a photo from the actual day in question? If one was not available, why use an old one to deceive readers? What may have been an attempt to end rumors simply led to more.

Another example of an image that spread rapidly is the image of the Fukushima flowers, earlier mentioned as part of the Stanford media literacy study. One image with a claim about nuclear radiation spread like wildfire and was accepted as truth. Experts say that it is impossible to tell if the unusual flowers were affected by radiation. Most believe the flowers show a natural mutation.

But how exactly do these images and stories spread so quickly? It is a matter of pressing a button to send or share, but why do some become so popular? To understand this, we need to look at memes.

A Closer Look at Memes

A meme is an image, video clip, or short piece of text that spreads via the internet and goes viral. Some memes may undergo changes with each share. Users may add their own caption to an image. Typically, they express an idea or thought that many other internet users will identify with, and therefore will be happy to share. One popular meme subject is Grumpy Cat. Images of the feline are often circulated with captions expressing disdain for something.

Another shows the actor Sean Bean as Boromir from the popular *Lord of the Rings* movies. It takes a fragment of his dialogue from the movie, "One does not simply ..." and the creator can simply add a new ending.

Professor Richard Dawkins introduced the idea of the meme in the 1970s.

Although memes have been made popular by the internet, they are not new. The idea of the meme was first introduced in the 1970s by biologist Richard Dawkins. He created the term from the Greek word *mimema*. It means something that is copied or imitated. Dawkins wanted to describe the way people share ideas or part of our popular culture. Memes and sharing them truly took off in the digital age. Now most internet users recognize and have probably shared many popular images such as the baby making a fist or the smiling dog.

Dawkins compares the meme to our own genetic material, saying that it will adapt and evolve like our genes. The strong memes, or DNA, survive and go on to be shared and reproduced. Weaker DNA and less popular memes fade away.

Researchers have found that shorter is better for a meme to become popular. As we spend more time browsing the internet, we spend less time actually looking at any one thing in depth. A meme has to get its point across quickly and easily to grab our attention. In the same way, a successful hoax or fake news story will often use a short, punchy headline, knowing that many readers will share on the basis that the headline will catch someone's eye, not the content.

Just as any meme needs multiple shares to thrive, so an internet hoax requires shares to be successful—which raises the question of motivation. There are many reasons people create a false story or piece of false information. Earlier in this chapter, we mentioned that some sites based on a fictional person or location are created by fans or are used to help sell a book. Now we turn our attention to other reasons for creating a hoax site. Often the motivation falls into one of two categories: economic or promotion of a specific cause, political or otherwise.

Hoaxes That "Pay Off"

Websites typically make money from advertising. Ads are placed on the site and sometimes within the text of the story. When readers click on the link to the advertisement,

You May Like   Sponsored Links by Taboola

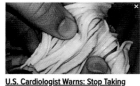

U.S. Cardiologist Warns: Stop Taking
Probiotics Immediately
Gundry MD

See The Face Mask That Drew
Barrymore Says Changed Her Life
Town and Country I Hanacure

3 Ways Your Dog Asks For Help
Dr. Marty

When studying a news site, look out for clickbait.

the site owner earns money, usually just a few cents.
More clicks equal more money, and so the goal is to get
as many people as possible to go to your site and follow
the links. This is known as clickbait. Clickbait's purpose
is to get you to click on the links. Often, this is done by
using outrageous headlines or false photos. The content
matters much less than whether it is eye-catching enough
to attract people. For those who run successful hoax sites,
the financial rewards from advertising can be impressive.
The owners of some smaller parody news sites say they
earn about $1,000 a month from advertising. The people
behind one fake news site earned more than $40,000 per
month by making up false political stories before the 2016
presidential election.

Recently, social media sites such as Facebook and
Twitter have introduced stricter rules to minimize the
spread of fake news. In 2015, the Pew Research Center
found that 63 percent of Americans get most of their
news from social media. Therefore, it makes sense for

WHAT ARE BOTS?

Bots are computer programs that are designed to perform all sorts of automatic tasks, from searching on the internet to something as simple as setting an alarm on your phone. The bots that made headlines during the 2016 presidential election are programs that set up fake Twitter and Facebook accounts. They act and look just like any other account. They like and share posts, and so on. But they do as they are programmed to do, and so they can help to spread hoaxes and other fake news.

Since the 2016 presidential election, bots created by programmers in Russia have been blamed for spreading false stories about some candidates. Thousands of these fake accounts might start tweeting about a topic. Other internet users will see and share, particularly if it matches their own beliefs. Soon the hoax will have become viral and widely believed to be true by many.

Following the election and a widespread outcry, many fake accounts were removed by social media in an attempt to stop the spreading of hoaxes. However, it is important to note that not all social media bots spread false news. Some can provide important information when it is needed. For example, one bot-based Twitter account sends automated messages in real time about any earthquake alerts in the San Francisco area.

hoaxers to make their stories as popular as possible on these channels.

The other motivation for many hoaxes and fake news stories is to promote a particular cause or viewpoint. During the 2016 election season, accusations of fake news flew in all directions, and the internet seemed to provide a never-ending stream of articles that could fit anyone's views, no matter how extreme. Thousands of fake social media accounts, known as bots, from Russia helped to spread falsehoods in an attempt to influence the results of the presidential election. Headlines went viral in a matter of minutes. Stories appeared so quickly and in such huge numbers that it became difficult to know what was real and what was false. Readers would become enraged by a headline, accept it at face value, share, and move on to the next. As mentioned in the previous chapter, even when a story is later proven to be false, readers have already accepted it as truth and therefore continue to make judgments based upon what they had read.

This helps to explain why hoaxes, especially those about political issues, become so popular. Readers are bombarded with headlines and images. The story may be obviously false. Or readers may never look beyond the headline. But their own bias means that they want a particular story to be true because it reinforces their opinions. They will share it to both reinforce their own beliefs and to receive validation of those beliefs from others who share. This is called confirmation bias. We want to be right, and so we seek out news stories that confirm this. Each of us interprets information according to our own bias. One trick to spotting internet hoaxes is to recognize the writer's bias and our own.

Thinking It Through

The internet has made it easy for anyone and everyone to publish. That freedom comes with a downside: no quality control. Newspapers and magazines have editors and publishers who check material before it goes to print. Some websites also do—for example, those operated by the mainstream media. However, many sites have no fact-checker to verify them. This does not automatically mean that a story is false, but it does put a greater burden on readers to check for themselves. Unfortunately, as the Stanford study shows, many internet users, students included, do not know how to check an article. However, honing media literacy skills allows us to fight back against hoaxes.

Abraham Lincoln is used in some popular memes and has been credited with many fake quotes about internet usage!

Fighting
Internet
Hoaxes

The key to seeing through any type of false information online, whether it be a news article, a photo, or a fake quote, is to know where it comes from and who put it on the internet. You have to research sources. Even this simple step can go a long way in telling you whether you should believe something.

Tips for Spotting Hoaxes

Pay Attention to URLs

In the case of a website, there are several ways to check whether it is reputable. First, look at the actual web address, or URL. Some are instantly recognizable. For example, the home page for CNN is http://www.cnn.com

The web address or URL of this website
(www.abcnews.com.co) is a hint that it's a fake.

and the British Broadcasting Corporation (BBC) is
http://www.bbc.co.uk because it is based in the United
Kingdom. Other common endings might include .edu
for a site linked to a college or school, .net, or a country
code (.ca for Canada). Some spoof websites can be tricky
as they pretend to be part of a well-known or legitimate
site by mimicking parts of the URL. Watch out for minor
misspellings (Amzon instead of Amazon) and for additions
to common URL endings. Everybody recognizes the .com
ending, but if a site address ends with .com.co, be careful.
It is likely to be a spoof site. A very genuine-looking news
site was set up at http://www.abcnews.com.co. Even the
logo looked like that used by the news station. However, it
was, in fact, a fake site.

Many experts recommend looking to see who owns a web address. It is easy to do a domain search, and the results may reveal that the people behind the site are not who you expect.

Learn More About the Source

Another way to learn more about a site is to look at the "About Us" page. Any reputable site should have this information. It will tell you about the organization or company, and you might be able to get a feeling for any bias. Do their claims about themselves seem honest? Watch out for exaggerated claims, such as awards or associations that sound fake. Satire site the *Onion* claims that it began "as a print newspaper in 1756" and "now enjoys a daily readership of 4.3 trillion." If in doubt, do a quick search on the award or association to see if it is real. Some humor or spoof sites will reveal on the "About Us" page that their material is indeed meant for entertainment only.

Next, look to see what else is on the site. If you have clicked on a link about a health topic, are the other stories on the site based on health and medicine? Do they look believable? If the other stories look fake, this one probably is too.

Check the Byline

It's important to look at who has written the story. Usually, a reputable news site will put the name of the journalist in the byline at the top of the article. Often, you can click on the person's name to see what else he or she has written. If not, you can do a search for the person's name. Sometimes, no byline is given. This is not always a warning sign; some pieces at major news publications are written by people on staff and there is no byline. Or sometimes the author will use a pseudonym (a fake name). This is more common if they are reporting from an area where they may be in danger if they are revealed as a journalist (perhaps a war zone). Sometimes the author will be listed as anonymous. This, in itself, is not a sign that a piece is untrue. It is part of a larger puzzle. You must put all the pieces together. An anonymous piece on a reputable site with proper links is likely to be trustworthy. An anonymous piece on a site with an odd URL and a lot of other attention-grabbing headlines should be a red flag.

Examine the Headline

The headline of a story is meant to catch your eye and make you want to read more. The headline of a hoax story is meant to catch your eye and make you share it with others. Today, we have access to so much breaking news, on TV and online, that many people believe the media will do anything to get attention. In fact, proper journalistic practice follows a style guide and is quite strict about what is presented and how. Be aware of the types of headlines used by hoax sites. Remember that this is clickbait. Clickbait creators want people to click on the link and then go to the advertisements so they can make money. Is the headline in all capitals (the equivalent of shouting on the internet)? Is it followed by numerous exclamation

Celebrity deaths are a common news hoax. This death hoax is on a fake site designed to mimic the BBC.

marks? One especially popular practice is to make it seem as if you are about to learn a great secret: "What They Don't Want You to Know About ..." or "Here's the REAL Reason Why You Should ... !!!!!!!" Another common hoax, sometimes simply spread via social media and sometimes used as clickbait, is the celebrity death hoax. If it is being used as clickbait, you will often see a picture of the celebrity with a caption such as "We All Miss ..." or "The Sad Truth About ..."

One last point about advertising is that many news pages will feature a mix of proper news stories, clear advertising, and sponsored content. The advertising and sponsored content is an additional way to make money and to prevent the news from being hidden behind a paywall, meaning that only paid subscribers have access. This doesn't necessarily mean that the news stories are not true. Treat them as you would any other news story, paying careful attention. It does mean, however, that you should become familiar with the differences between the types of content.

Read, Read, Read

The News Literacy Project (NLP) gives another useful tip for spotting hoaxes: How do you react to seeing the headline? Does it make you very angry? Are you very keen for it to be true, no matter how unlikely? If the goal is to get you to share a piece, to make it go viral, and to plant the seed in people's minds that something has happened, even when it hasn't, then the headline wants you to have a strong reaction to it. Too many people see a headline and share without reading any further. Of course, that brings us to the next important tip. Read more than just the headline. All too often, the actual story might be quite different than what you expect. Read before you share.

Seeing Through Hoaxes in All Forms

The next tips for seeing through hoaxes apply not just to a news story or an internet site. They also apply to other forms of online hoaxes, such as Photoshopped images and fake quotations.

Evaluating Memes

A popular series of memes on the internet shows a picture of Abraham Lincoln and a quote that is attributed to him. The quotes vary, but are all similar in nature: "The problem with quotes found on the internet is that they are often not true." "If it's on the internet, it must be true." Obviously these are fake and President Lincoln never said any such thing. They do, however, point to a larger problem: fake quotations. They are everywhere, not just in news articles but in memes. People love inspirational quotations, but all too often, the person in the meme did not say what is being attributed to them. Abraham Lincoln is a beloved figure in US history, and so claiming that he said something may make it seem more genuine. Quite the opposite is often true. And so, while some of these memes may be entertaining, do not accept them at face value. If in doubt, do a search for the quote to find who originally said it. Be warned: this can sometimes be difficult. The more popular the quote and meme, the more frequently it has been wrongly attributed. Despite what you may see on social media, President Taft did not say, "Speak softly and carry a big stick." (That was President Theodore Roosevelt.) Nor was author John Green the first to say, "You miss 100% of the shots you don't take." (The origin of that quote is still rather vague, with some giving credit to Wayne Gretzky and others saying its origin is lost to history.)

Photos, GIFs, and Videos

Then there is the matter of fake photos, GIFs, and videos. Images that have been altered are not a new concept. Before the era of the internet, many cheap weekly

WHEN SCIENCE IS MISREPORTED

Did you hear the one about how eating french fries can cure baldness? Several international newspapers reported it! Sadly, the idea that french fries can grow your hair back is absolutely false. This is just another example of how medical research can be misinterpreted.

In November 2017, a report appeared in a biomedical magazine explaining how Japanese scientists had been able to use a particular substance to grow hair follicles in a laboratory. They think that this could one day be a useful method of hair transplantation.

A few months later, a story in a British newspaper announced that fries from a certain well-known fast food restaurant could cure baldness and regrow hair. So how did they reach that conclusion? The most likely explanation is that someone saw parts of the study and realized that the substance used is also used in the cooking of fries. They

French fries won't cure baldness, but many people thought it might after a hoax spread.

then concluded that eating fries must regrow hair in the same way that scientists could in a petri dish. Although a rather funny story, it does show how misinterpreting scientific reports can lead to huge misunderstandings, sometimes with much more serious consequences.

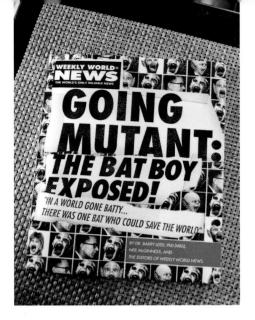

Headlines about Bat Boy were meant to be entertaining, not to provide real news.

publications would draw attention and readers by having bad, obviously doctored (or altered to deceive the viewer) photos on their front covers. A memorable example is Bat Boy on the cover of the *Weekly World News*. People knew that these images and the stories that accompanied them were fake, but they were entertaining. In the same way, there are some photo hoaxes on the internet that are simply entertaining. Others can be more misleading.

As mentioned in the last chapter, modern technology makes it very easy to change a photo. With a few clicks of a button, you can change the color of someone's eyes, change the background of the photo, and put something in the person's hand. Don't believe everything you see. Some photos have obviously been altered. They are either too absurd to be true or they have not been expertly done. You might be able to tell that someone else's face has been pasted on, for example. Others are much more skillfully done, and these can be difficult to detect. Studies show that fewer and fewer people are able to spot a doctored (or fake) photo.

It is now easier
than ever to change
details on a
photograph.

Don't forget that a close look at a picture might reveal some details that seem a little odd. Is there snow in the background of that picture that claims to be in Brazil? Does one of the people seem to be oddly positioned compared to everyone else? Shadows or reflections in the wrong place can be an easy sign that something has been changed. If you look at an image and feel that something isn't quite right, try zooming in closer. That can sometimes reveal where the hoaxer has erased a detail or added something that shouldn't be there.

If the photo is genuine, it may still be mislabeled. Be cautious of any image or video that does not have information about who took it and when. There are tools you can use to find out if the image has been used on the internet before. In March 2014, a photo appeared on Twitter showing soldiers dragging a man's body through the street. It was accompanied by the caption, "Homosexual stoned by police in Uganda." It was quickly shared and commented on as people denounced the violence in the African nation. But one response was from a journalist. He recognized the image since it had appeared in a British newspaper just one month earlier. The photo was, in fact, from the Central African Republic. The dead man was not homosexual but a suspected militiaman. Nevertheless, despite the journalist's correction, the photo with the incorrect caption was already being widely shared and believed. The damage was done. The incorrect caption may have been unintentional, but it was misleading.

A simple reverse image search could have prevented such a mistake. Reverse search engines can tell you where an image originated. They can be a valuable tool in spotting an internet hoax. Sites such as TinEye (http://www.tineye.com) or Google's reverse-photo search (https://reverse.photos) allow the user to drag and drop an image, or to paste the web address. The search engine then scours the internet, finding where the image has appeared before. You may find that a photo about an event that happened yesterday was actually taken five years ago!

Understanding Fact-Checking

If a lot of mainstream media sources are reporting something, it is more likely to be true. If something is only appearing on sites sharing the same bias, it might be worth checking the facts before sharing. Comparing with other sites is a worthwhile tip, even for information or media not found on social media. From checking a quote or an image to seeing if a site's medical advice is accurate, always do a search to see where else the information can be found.

Luckily, there are now many reputable fact-checking sites that can help in the task of investigating a hoax. In the 1990s, a website called Snopes started debunking popular urban legends, cultural myths, and similar hoax stories. Since then, it has grown to become the most widely used and one of the most respected fact-checking sites. It is an excellent place to start on a fact-checking quest, whether you are wondering about a particular ghost story, if a politician really did say that quotation, or if a celebrity really has died.

Another well-respected site is FactCheck.org. Part of the University of Pennsylvania's Annenberg Public Policy Center, FactCheck.org provides detailed analyses of current political stories as well as medical and scientific reports.

Conquering Media Literacy

As computer technologies become more advanced and more readily available, it is becoming easier than ever to create and spread realistic hoaxes. Knowing where to begin seeking the truth can seem quite overwhelming. However, there are also many available tools designed to help internet users spot hoaxes. The advice given in this chapter comes from experienced journalists, librarians, and fact-checking organizations. When you first begin learning media literacy, you may think there are many complicated steps to follow. The more you use them, the more skilled you will become. Eventually, you will be able to recognize an inaccurate headline or a misused image quite easily.

FIGHTING FAKE NEWS ON FACEBOOK

Social media outlets such as Twitter and Facebook have been widely criticized for their part in spreading hoaxes and other fake news. In 2017, during US Senate hearings, the companies were told that they should have done a better job of identifying and stopping Russian accounts and advertisements that were intended to sway voters during the 2016 presidential election. As a result, Facebook implemented new plans to try to prevent the spread of such hoaxes.

Previous attempts to discourage false news had allowed users to dispute stories. The disputed pieces were then investigated by two fact-checkers. However, the process was very slow and ineffective. Facebook decided to abandon the scheme. Now, when users click on a link in their News Feed, they also see links to other outlets that have reported the same story. The goal is to allow readers to see other perspectives on the news, helping them to decide if it is true or false.

Since many false news stories were being spread through advertising, Facebook also said in January 2018 that they were changing what would appear in people's feeds. People now see less marketing and more news from friends.

These students are studying journalism. Media literacy skills are important for both those who write the news and those who read it.

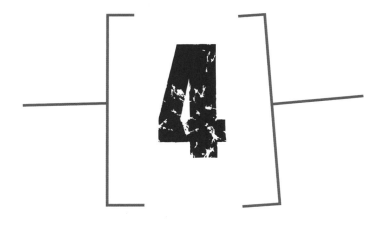

Putting Your Skills into Action

I t is time to put what we have learned into practice. This chapter will look at three stories that have proven popular on the internet and show step-by-step how to prove if they are true or false.

Hercules, the World's Largest Dog?

Everyone seems to love sharing a cute dog photo or cat video, and so internet users everywhere were excited to see Hercules the giant dog. Several different but similar photos of these giant canines have been shared over the years. Perhaps the most famous shows a woman walking her horse and chatting with a man walking his dog. The dog is nearly as large as the horse. The picture claims to show Hercules, the world's largest dog. The English mastiff apparently weighs 282 pounds (128 kilograms). Are there really dogs this big? If so, how have we never seen one in person?

This seemingly giant dog is another example of how photos can be manipulated.

This image appeared on many social media sites, but no one seemed to know who the people in the photo were. If Hercules is so big, who is his owner? Where was the picture taken? These should be warnings that it might not be real. You might even do a search for a giant dog called Hercules. The best hoaxes have an element of truth in them, and this one is no different. There was indeed an English mastiff called Hercules who weighed 282 pounds (128 kg). A search for him and his owner shows that both the real Hercules and his owner look quite different from the person and dog in the photo. Mastiffs are big dogs. However, if we do a little research about them, we would learn that even the biggest of the breed grows to a maximum height of about 30 inches (76 centimeters). That is much shorter than what is shown.

Hercules is indeed a real dog, but the dog in the photo is not the real Hercules. The photo has been digitally altered. Any dog that was truly that big would weigh almost 1,000 pounds (454 kg)! The photo is funny to look at but definitely fake.

Amina Arraf: Fact or Fiction?

Some hoaxes can be funny. Some are more serious. Sometimes they even fool the mainstream media. One example is the case of Amina Arraf. She was a Syrian American woman who lived in Damascus, Syria. For six years, she wrote a blog about her life as a persecuted gay woman in the Middle East and the various political uprisings that were happening. She wrote about the violent anti-government protests and about how her own life was in danger because of her sexuality. She quickly developed a strong following, especially among journalists who relied on bloggers and writers in the Middle East to keep them updated on current affairs. Arraf was interviewed via email many times. A book about her life was being planned.

In June 2011, Arraf's cousin posted on the blog. Arraf had been kidnapped and her family feared for her life. Newspapers such as the *Guardian* and the *New York Times* reported the story, in print and online. People set up campaigns to raise awareness and to help find her. There was just one problem. Amina Arraf did not exist.

WHEN HOAXES BECOME DANGEROUS: PIZZAGATE

A fake news story, even one that seems far-fetched, can lead to a very dangerous situation. One such example is the story of Pizzagate.

During the presidential election in 2016, many false stories were being spread online as "fact." In late October, someone posted on Facebook, claiming to have information about presidential candidate Hillary Clinton's involvement with a network that was abusing and trafficking young girls. The girls were reportedly being held in the basement of Comet Ping Pong, a pizza restaurant in Washington, DC. The story quickly spread on Twitter and other social media outlets, and soon it was being reported by several conservative media outlets.

Meanwhile, the pizzeria (which did not even have a basement) started to receive repeated threats of violence against its staff. On December 4, 2016, a man walked into the restaurant with an AR-15 and fired three shots. Luckily, no one was injured and the man was arrested. He told police that he was investigating the crime so that he could rescue the children. He was later sentenced to four years in prison.

Journalists who investigated the story later found that thousands of people had played a part in spreading the hoax. It shows the danger of sharing stories that have not been properly verified. It also shows how quickly something can take on a life of its own via the internet.

Even well-regarded mainstream newspapers fall for hoaxes sometimes. The *Guardian* reported on Amina Arraf's kidnapping, not realizing that she did not exist.

This elaborate hoax was the work of a middle-aged American man living in Scotland. He said that he wanted to draw attention to people's struggles in the Middle East. Thanks to an NPR journalist, the hoax unraveled. As the journalist read the stories, something occurred to him. All of the reporters and people who thought they knew Arraf had never actually met her, or even spoken to her. All of her communications had been via email. Some supporters had developed close friendships with her over the months and were horrified to learn that they had been duped and were, in fact, chatting online with an American man instead of an Arab woman.

While the NPR journalist and several bloggers were uncovering the truth, a woman from London called one of the newspapers to ask why her Facebook photo had been used in a story about a kidnapped woman. The American Embassy said they had no record of someone matching Amina's description with both American and Syrian passports.

The perpetrator of the hoax eventually came forward and admitted he had made everything up. He denied that he had done anything wrong, but many disagreed, saying that he may have put some activists and women in Syria in danger.

Although so many people were fooled by this hoax, it is important to notice the details that revealed it to be false. The photo was not really Arraf. A reverse image search might have led to the real person's social media accounts. There were no real records of Arraf existing. All of the evidence existed online and nowhere else.

Every hoax or fake news story contains enough true information to make it believable. In both the Hercules and Amina Arraf examples, there was a certain grain of truth that made people want to believe them. There really was a giant dog called Hercules. The struggles of people in Syria were being reported online, so why wouldn't we want to read the blog of one person living through these terrible events? Those grains of truth are then distorted into something else: a Photoshopped image, a stolen Facebook photo, an entirely fictitious person. However, by carefully checking the information, people were able to reveal both hoaxes.

The Case of Nancy Markle and Aspartame

One final hoax example dates back to the early days of internet use, when fewer people were familiar with the web. In the 1990s, a letter started circulating via email and newsgroups. The writer, going by the name of Nancy Markle, claimed to be a scientist who had recently spoken at the World Environmental Conference about the dangers of aspartame, a popular sugar substitute. She made many claims, including that the sweetener caused multiple sclerosis and lupus. At the time, as mentioned, the internet was quite young. Few people knew how to use it or how to check the information they were reading. The information spread, and even now, some twenty years later, you are likely to find websites stating that aspartame will cause these diseases. The US Food and Drug Administration has

The idea that aspartame caused lupus and multiple sclerosis started with a fake story in the 1990s, and many still believe the story's claims.

repeatedly denied the claims, but as with so many hoaxes, the rumor persists.

Following the steps covered in this book will reveal the hoax fairly easily. You might do a search for the scientist by name. You would find that no such person exists. You might also search for information about the conference, which should have its own web page, schedule, and links to speakers. Again, you would find no evidence of any such conference. You might also check reputable medical sites or medical journals online. Such an important medical discovery would be discussed by doctors and scientists around the world. One last clue would be the way that the email is written. It is badly written and contains a lot of capitalized words. Remember that this is a common trick

THE NEWS LITERACY PROJECT

The News Literacy Project was founded in 2008 by Alan Miller. He was a journalist with the *Los Angeles Times* and was inspired after speaking about his work to a class

of sixth-graders. Miller realized that people are exposed to so many news sources today that it can be confusing to know what to believe. He wanted to create an organization where journalists could explain what they do to students. The project allows students to better understand news stories. It also teaches them tools to evaluate stories and to spot hoaxes and other fake news.

Many major news organizations have become partners of the News Literacy Project. They send volunteers to speak to middle- and high-school students in the larger cities. In 2016, the NLP also launched an online program so that students around the country can learn from them. The Checkology Virtual Classroom provides interactive lessons that guide learners through social media and digital news platforms. It teaches how to filter information and about the importance of quality journalism. By February 2018, teachers from across the United States and all around the world had registered for the Checkology Virtual Classroom, reaching an estimated 1.78 million students.

used by clickbait and fake headlines. Twenty years ago, many internet users would not have been able to check the information provided. Today, a few simple searches should give you all the answers you need.

Putting It All Together

Carefully checking the information is key to developing media literacy. When coming across some information that you might want to share online, take a few minutes first to think about whether it is truthful:

- Check who wrote the article or took the photo.
- Check the website address.
- Check the who, when, and where.
- Read beyond the headline.
- If in doubt, use a reputable online fact-checking site.

Every day, we are constantly bombarded with information: advertisements, news stories, health advice, and all of those entertaining little things like funny memes and videos. Some are harmless jokes, while others are designed to try to make us think a certain way, to buy a particular item, or to click a specific link. It is vital to be informed and to know what is going on in the world. It is equally vital to think critically and to recognize bias, inaccurate information, and misleading opinions. By developing media literacy skills, you can learn to solve puzzles, search for answers, and to see through the internet hoaxes you find.

GLOSSARY

bots Also known as web robots or internet robots, bots are a piece of software that run an automated task.

byline The line in a news article that tells us who wrote the article. It is usually found underneath the headline.

citizen journalism Reporting carried out by everyday people, not by professional journalists.

clickbait Internet content links that are designed to attract attention and get users to click on them.

cognitive ability The mental skills that we use to do any type of task. This includes our ability to pay attention to something and to solve a problem.

confirmation bias The way that a person typically processes and analyzes information according to one's own beliefs.

fringe group People with ideas and theories that are not mainstream.

headline The main title at the top of a news story that is in bigger print than the rest of the text. It should tell you what the story is about.

hoax A trick or falsehood that may be intended as a practical joke or as deliberately cruel.

malicious Intended to hurt or do harm to someone.

media literacy The ability to view many types of media (internet, newspapers, images, and so on) and to evaluate them for accuracy and bias.

meme An image, GIF, or video that makes a reference to popular culture. It is meant to be shared, and many become viral.

satire A type of commentary on current events or society. It usually makes use of humor and/or exaggeration to poke fun at a topic.

social media Websites that allow users to share news, images, and other content with friends, family, and other followers. Examples include Facebook, Twitter, and Instagram.

sponsored content A type of advertising that presents information as in a news story but which is intended to sell you a certain product.

unsubstantiated Something that has no evidence to support it.

validation Accepting something as true.

viral Internet content that is shared quickly and gains a large following.

FURTHER INFORMATION

BOOKS

Pascoe, Elaine, and Laurie Keller. *Fooled You!: Fakes and Hoaxes Through the Years*. New York: Square Fish Books, 2016.

Pattison, Darcy, and Peter Willis. *The Nantucket Sea Monster: A Fake News Story*. Little Rock, AR: Mims House, 2017.

WEBSITES

FactCheck.org
https://www.factcheck.org

This organization monitors political news, interviews, and advertising, and checks for accuracy. The site also provides fact-checking reports on science and health news.

News Literacy Project
http://www.thenewsliteracyproject.org

Find tools, tips, and resources for teachers and students to learn how to separate fact from fiction in news stories.

Snopes
https://www.snopes.com

Founded in 1994, Snopes is widely considered the leading source for fact-checking and debunking internet hoaxes. The site is a favorite among journalists, researchers, and internet users.

VIDEOS

How to Choose Your News
https://ed.ted.com/lessons/how-to-choose-your-news-damon-brown

This talk by Damon Brown is from the TED-Ed Talk series and shares tips on how to tell the difference between opinion and fact in the news.

How to Detect Baloney, Carl Sagan Style
https://www.facebook.com/BigThinkScience/videos/1440081122770674

Writer Michael Sherman gives ten tips for how to debunk science hoaxes. The advice is equally applicable for approaching online material and for developing critical thinking skills.

How to Spot Fake News
https://www.youtube.com/watch?v=AkwWcHekMdo

This animated video from FactCheck.org discusses fake news and provides sensible advice for analyzing information that you find online.

BIBLIOGRAPHY

Barthel, Michael, Elisa Shearer, Jeffrey Gottfried, and Amy
    Mitchell. "The Evolving Role of News on Twitter and
    Facebook." Pew Research Center, July 2015. http://
    www.journalism.org/2015/07/14/the-evolving-role-of-
    news-on-twitter-and-facebook.

BBC. "The Saga of 'Pizzagate': The Fake Story That Shows
    How Conspiracy Theories Spread." December 2, 2016.
    http://www.bbc.com/news/blogs-trending-38156985.

Davis, Wynne. "Fake or Real? How to Self-Check
    the News and Get the Facts." NPR, December
    5, 2016. https://www.npr.org/sections/
    alltechconsidered/2016/12/05/503581220/fake-or-real-
    how-to-self-check-the-news-and-get-the-facts.

Domonoske, Camila. "Students Have 'Dismaying' Inability
    to Tell Fake News From Real, Study Finds." NPR,
    November 23, 2016. https://www.npr.org/sections/
    thetwo-way/2016/11/23/503129818/study-finds-
    students-have-dismaying-inability-to-tell-fake-news-
    from-real.

Hambrick, David Z., and Madeline Marquardt.
    "Cognitive Ability and Vulnerability to Fake News."
    Scientific American, February 6, 2018. https://
    www.scientificamerican.com/article/cognitive-

ability-and-vulnerability-to-fake-news/?utm_
source=facebook&utm_medium=social&utm_
campaign=sa-editorial-social&utm_content&utm_
term=mind_news.

Joseph, Ray. "Guide: How to Spot Fakes and Hoaxes
Online." *Africa Check*, April 23, 2014. https://
africacheck.org/factsheets/guide-how-to-spot-fakes-
and-hoaxes-online.

Paschal, Maureen. "This School Librarian Teaches Students
About (Actual) Fake News. Here's How Parents Can,
Too." *Washington Post*, December 27, 2017. https://www.
washingtonpost.com/news/parenting/wp/2017/12/27/
this-school-librarian-teaches-her-students-about-
actual-fake-news-heres-how-parents-can-too/?utm_
term=.d34933dda763.

Piper, Paul S. "Better Read That Again: Web Hoaxes and
Misinformation." *Searcher* 8 (2000): 40–49.

Schulten, Katherine, and Amanda Christy Brown.
"Evaluating Sources in a 'Post-Truth' World: Ideas
for Teaching and Learning About Fake News." *New
York Times*, January 19, 2017. https://www.nytimes.
com/2017/01/19/learning/lesson-plans/evaluating-
sources-in-a-post-truth-world-ideas-for-teaching-
and-learning-about-fake-news.html.

INDEX

ABOUT THE AUTHOR

Fiona Young-Brown has written a number of books, including *Eleanor Roosevelt: First Lady*, *Nuclear Fusion and Fission*, and *Edward Snowden: Contractor and Whistle-Blower*. She also enjoys writing about food, travel, and great apes. Originally from England, Young-Brown now lives in Kentucky with her husband and two dogs.